Water Power

Ed Catherall

Young Scientist

First published in 1981 by Wayland (Publishers) Limited
49 Lansdowne Place, Hove, East Sussex BN3 1HF, England
© Copyright 1981 Wayland (Publishers) Limited
ISBN 0 85340 870 X

Second impression 1983
Third impression 1984

Illustrated by Ted Draper
Designed and typeset by DP Press Limited, Sevenoaks, Kent
Printed in Italy by G. Canale & C.S.p.A., Turin

Contents

Looking at water

Fill a clear glass with tap water.
Look through the glass.
What can you see?
What is the colour of your tap water?
What can you smell in your tap water?
What taste has your tap water?
Dip your fingers in the tap water.
How do your fingers feel?
Rub your wet finger and thumb
together.
Notice how your finger and thumb
slide over each other.

Look at the surface of the water.
What can you see?
What happens to the water surface
as it touches the glass?

Tilt the glass. What happens to the surface of the water?
Line the surface up with a horizontal bar on a window.
Tilt the glass. Can you keep the surface of the water
in line with the horizontal bar?

Fill a glass tube with water.
Cork the tube so that a small
bubble of air can be seen.
Tilt the tube. What happens to the
air bubble?
You have made a level.
Use your level to check that
horizontal things really are level.

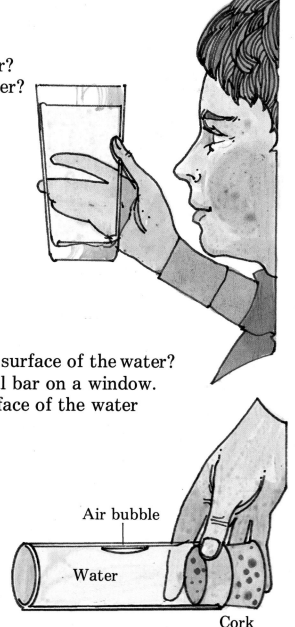

Air bubble

Water

Cork

4

Water levels and fountains

Join two plastic funnels together with a
clear plastic tube.
Hold the funnels side by side.
Ask a friend to pour water into one
funnel.
What happens?
Where are the water levels?
Slowly raise one funnel.
What happens?

Two
funnels

Plastic tube

Replace one of the funnels with the jet
of a dropper.
Hold the dropper jet level with the
funnel.
Are the water levels the same?
Raise the dropper jet. What happens?

Slowly raise the funnel.
What happens to the water in the
dropper jet?
Have you made a fountain?

Raise your funnel 10 cm above your
dropper jet.
How high a fountain do you get?

What is the highest fountain jet that
you can make?

Dropper

Water finds its own level

Put a funnel into a length of clear
plastic tubing.
Put the other end of the tubing in a jar.
Slowly pour water into the funnel
until the jar is nearly full.
Pinch the tubing near the funnel.
Remove the funnel.
Put the pinched end of the tubing
into a second jar.
What happens?
You have made a siphon.
Lift one jar.
What happens to the water levels?
Which way is the water flowing?
What happens if you lift the tube
out of the water?
What happens if you get air in the
tubing?

Remove one end of the tube from
its jar. Lower this end of the tube
and see how the water runs out.
Quickly, bend the tube into a
'U' shape before all of the
water runs out. What happens?
Does the water keep running out?

You have made a water trap.
Are water levels in the U-bend the
same?
This U-bend is similar to the trap in
a sink waste pipe.

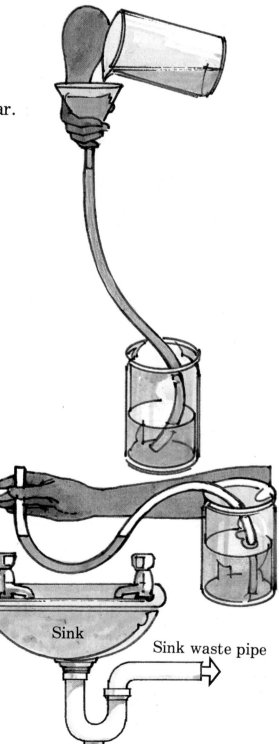

Sink

Sink waste pipe

Chapter 2 Uses of water power

A water-powered wheel

Find a straight cork which is shorter than the diameter of a plastic bottle.
Cut four slits at right angles in the cork.
Push a metal knitting needle through the centre of the cork.

Cut a window out of one side of a plastic bottle.
From the window plastic cut four equal strips.
Push these strips into the cork.

Make two holes in the bottle above the window.
Place your wheel through the window and push the needle through each hole and the cork.

See that the needle spins freely.
Stop the needle from coming out by fixing cork washers to each end.

Make a hole in the base of the bottle and push it onto a tap.
Slowly run water into your bottle.
Does water fall onto the paddles?
How fast does your water wheel turn?
What happens when you increase the water flow?

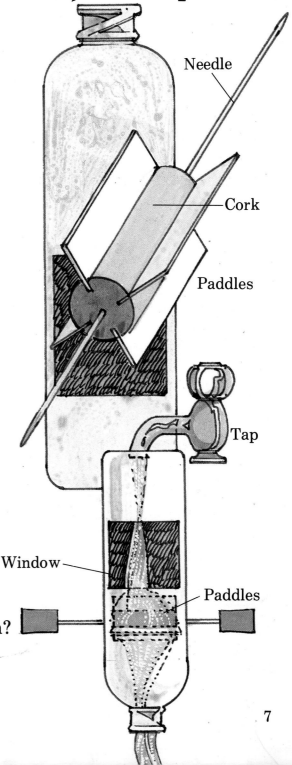

Needle

Cork

Paddles

Tap

Window

Paddles

Mills driven by water power

Centuries ago, water mills or grist mills were built on the banks of streams to grind cereal to flour.

These mills had huge paddle wheels.

The water turned the wheel which was connected through gear wheels to the grindstones. If the water fell on the wheel, it was called an overshot wheel.

If the wheel was placed in a fast flowing stream, it was called an undershot wheel.

In both mills, the miller built a dam across the stream. This controlled the flow of water, so that he could control the speed of the wheel. Grindstones need to turn fairly slowly.

Head of water

Water power makes electricity

Water turbines are used to make electricity.
This is called hydro-electric power.
Hydro is the Greek word for water.
Turbines are water wheels that usually turn horizontally, rather than vertically as in a water mill. The water needs to be travelling fast in order to turn the turbine fast. The faster the turbine spins, the more electricity is made.
Hydro-electric power stations are placed near dams or at the bottom of waterfalls.

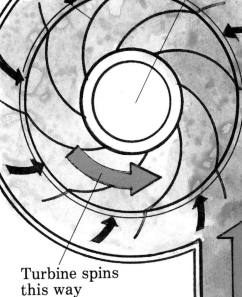

Water outlet

Turbine blades

Turbine spins this way

Water in

If there is no convenient waterfall, we can still generate electrical power from water.
We heat the water in a pipe and turn it to steam.
Because steam takes up 1750 times more volume than the same amount of water, a great pressure is produced in the pipe.
So steam is produced as a powerful jet that turns the blades of the turbine.
To heat the water, we burn oil or coal or use nuclear power.

Making a paddleboat

Cut out a boat shape from balsa wood.
Cut a square out of the stern for the paddle drive.

Cut two identical paddles.
Notch the centre of each paddle.
Fit them together to form a cross.

Use a strong rubber band to fix the
paddles to the boat.
Notch the sides of the boat to keep
the rubber bands in place.

Wind up your paddle.
Hold the paddle and place your boat in water.
How far will your boat go?
What happens if you wind your paddle the other way?
How can you make your boat go faster and further?
Moving water can turn a wheel and the wheel can
produce power.
Or, power can turn a wheel to move water.

Making a propeller-driven boat

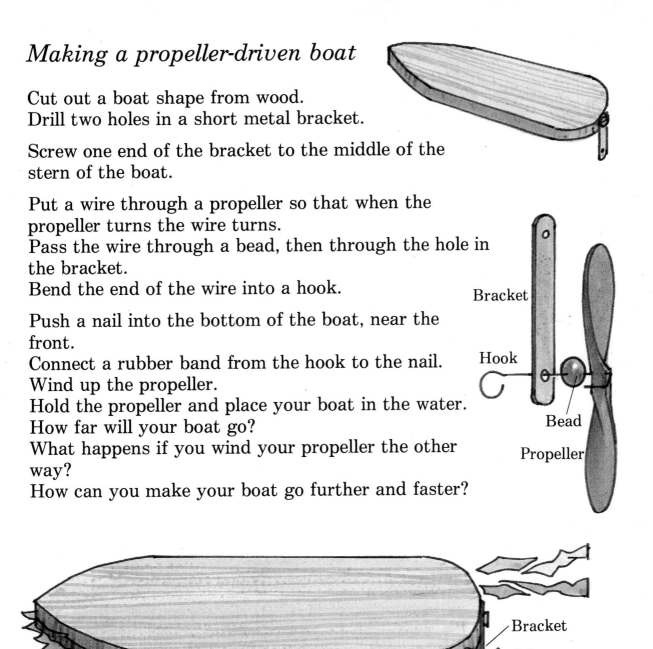

Cut out a boat shape from wood.
Drill two holes in a short metal bracket.

Screw one end of the bracket to the middle of the
stern of the boat.

Put a wire through a propeller so that when the
propeller turns the wire turns.
Pass the wire through a bead, then through the hole in
the bracket.
Bend the end of the wire into a hook.

Push a nail into the bottom of the boat, near the
front.
Connect a rubber band from the hook to the nail.
Wind up the propeller.
Hold the propeller and place your boat in the water.
How far will your boat go?
What happens if you wind your propeller the other
way?
How can you make your boat go further and faster?

Bracket

Hook

Bead

Propeller

Bracket

Propeller

Rubber band

Nail

Making a steam-powered boat

Find a cork that will fit tightly into a metal cigar tube.
Use a nail to make a small hole through the cork.

Wind two lengths of strong wire around the cigar tube.
Make sure the wire holds the tube firmly.

Cut out a boat shape from balsa wood.
Place two stumps of candle side by side on the boat.
Fix the candles to the boat with hot wax.

Stick the ends of the wire into the top of the balsa boat.
Make sure that the cigar tube is over the candle wicks.

Push two nails into the bottom of the boat to act as a keel.

Quarter-fill the cigar tube with hot water.
Push the cork in tightly. Place the boat in water.
Light the candles.
What happens?
How far will your boat go?
When does it stop?

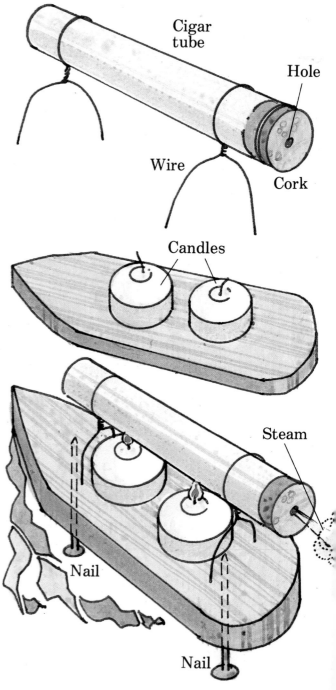

Making water-powered clocks

Find a plastic bottle with a nozzle. A washing-up-liquid bottle is ideal.
Fill the plastic bottle with water.
Turn it upside down.
Does any water come out of the nozzle?
Using a nail, make a small hole in the base of the bottle.
Now will water come out of the nozzle?
How long does it take for the bottle to empty?
Refill the bottle. Turn the bottle so that the water runs out of the other hole.
Does the bottle take the same amount of time to empty?

Use a hammer and a nail to punch a hole in the base of a large can.
Put your finger over the hole and fill the can with water.
How long does the can take to empty?
Does the water level fall at a steady rate?

Place your empty can upright in a large container of water.
How long does it take to sink?
Does it sink at a steady rate?
Did it take the same time to sink as it did to empty?
Weight the can with washers.
Record the effect of weight on the rate of sinking.

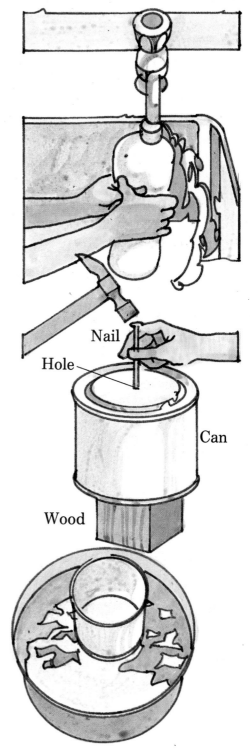

Nail

Hole

Can

Wood

A model Chinese water clock

Find six identical, clean plastic cups.
Make a small hole in the centre of the
base of five of the cups.
Mark a centimetre scale on the side of
the sixth cup.

Screw the five cups with holes in, one
above the other on a board.
Place the marked cup under the other
five.
Put your finger over the hole in the top
cup and fill it with water.
Take your finger away.
How long does it take for the first
drops of water to reach the bottom
cup?
How long does it take for the water
level in the bottom cup to reach 1 cm?
Mark the bottom cup with a time scale.
How could you make your clock go
slower?
What happens if you put a little liquid
detergent in the water?

Scale

Hole

Water pressure

Fill a plastic detergent bottle with water.
Replace the top and close the bottle.
Squeeze and feel how the water
resists you squeezing the bottle.
Open the bottle.
Aim the bottle at a sink or
bucket.
Squeeze the bottle gently, then
press hard.
Which pressure makes the
stronger jet of water?

Bucket

Holes

Put an empty can over a piece
of wood.
Use a nail to make a line of
holes up the side of the can.
Make each hole the same size
and make them the same
distance apart.
Cover the holes with a strip of
masking tape.
Fill the can with water.
Set the can above a bowl or
sink.
Quickly remove the tape.

Tape

Shelf

At which hole is the jet of water
strongest?
What happens to the jets as the
water level falls?

Bowl

15

Depth and water pressure

Put an empty can over a piece
of wood.
Use a nail to make a line of
holes at the base of the can.
Make each hole the same
distance from the top of the can.
Cover the holes with masking
tape.
Fill the can with water.
Set the can above a bowl or sink.
Quickly remove the tape.

Are the water jets the same?
What happens to the jets as the
water level falls?
Dry the outside of the can and
retape the holes.
Refill the can and tilt it.
What do you think will happen
when you remove the tape?
Remove the tape. Were you
right?

16

Using water-pressure power

Make a line of holes around the base of a can (page 16).
Make two holes at the top of the can.
Tie a length of fine, strong thread to the top two holes.
Tie another length of thread to the middle of this thread.

Cover the base holes with masking tape.
Fill the can with water.
Hold the can over a sink or bowl by the thread.
Quickly remove the tape.
What happens?

Put the nail back into each hole.
Push the nail over sharply to one side.
This will move the direction of the hole.
Try to adjust each hole in the same way.
Cover the holes with sticky tape.
Fill the can with water.
Hold the can by the thread.
Quickly remove the tape.
What happens to the water jets?
What happens to the can?
What happens when the can is empty?

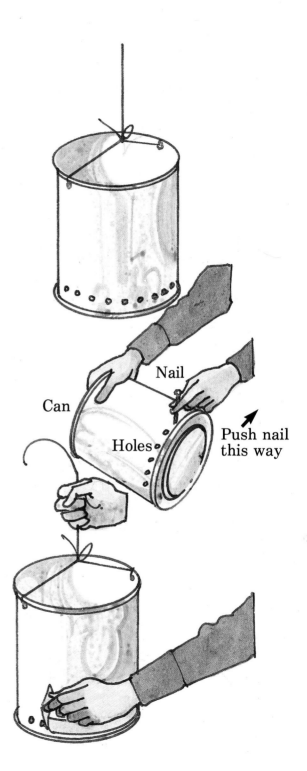

Can

Nail

Holes

Push nail
this way

Making a water-powered rocket

Find two identical plastic detergent bottles.
Make sure that they are clean.
Cut two rings from one bottle.
Cut three fin shapes from this bottle.

Put the two rings over the other plastic bottle.
Fit the three fins under the lower ring.
Place the fins an equal distance apart.

Connect a football-pump needle valve to a pump connector.
Tape the needle valve to a strong stick.
Place the stick firmly in the ground.
Point the stick away from people, buildings and trees.

Take out the rocket nozzle.
Quarter-fill the rocket with water.
Replace the nozzle.
Put your rocket on the needle valve.
See that the valve enters the nozzle.
Pump air quickly into your rocket.
Stand back as your rocket lifts off.
How far did your rocket go?

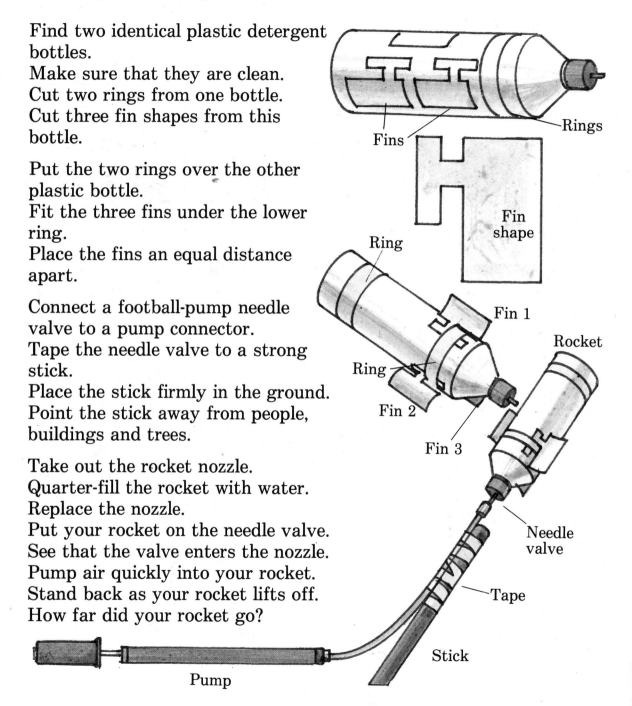

Fins
Rings
Fin shape
Ring
Fin 1
Rocket
Ring
Fin 2
Fin 3
Needle valve
Tape
Stick
Pump

Chapter 4 Water power shapes the land

Rain power

Stand outside in heavy rain.
Can you feel the force of the rain
drops on your hands and face?

Watch rain drops hitting a
puddle.
How do they splash?
Watch rain drops hitting soil.
What do the rain drops do to
the soil?
Find a place where rain drips
from a roof.
What happens to the soil here?
Sometimes you can find a
miniature waterfall.

Line a wooden box with plastic
sheeting.
Cut a hole through the box and
the plastic sheeting.
Fill your box with sandy soil.
Place your box on a slope.
Water the soil near the top
using a hose. What happens to
the soil?

How is the soil being moved?
What happens if you increase the slope of the soil?
What happens if you increase the water jet?
What happens if you use clay soil?

The power of stream water

Collect pictures of floods from newspapers.
Which rivers flooded?
How much damage was done?

Shake some soil in a jar of water.
What colour is the water?
Let the jar stand for two days.
What happens to the water?
What happens to the soil?
Where are the largest stones?
Go outside during heavy rain.
Where is the rain water going?
How is the soil being moved?

Hold a bendy branch in a fast-flowing, small, shallow stream.
What can you feel?
Use some corks to see how fast the water in the stream is moving.
Where does the stream water move fastest?
Where is the bank being worn away?
Where is the worn-away soil being deposited?

Water runoff

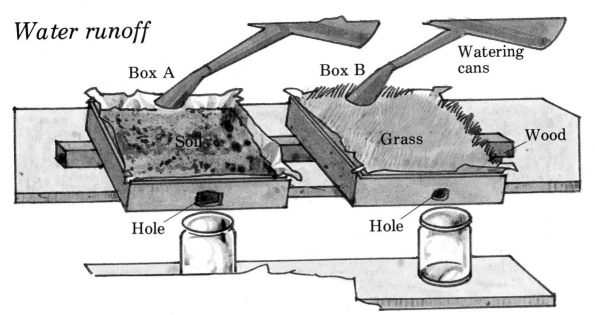

Box A   Box B   Watering cans

Soil   Grass   Wood

Hole   Hole

Find two identical wooden boxes.
Line both boxes with plastic sheeting.
Cut a hole in each box. Cut through the plastic.
Fill box A with soil.
Half-fill box B with soil, and cover the surface with turf.
Pack the soil down in box A.
Pack the turf down in box B.
Place both boxes on the same slope. Put a jar under each hole.
With a full watering can, water the grass at the top of box B. Empty the watering can.
Water box A at the top with the same amount of water.

What happens to the water in box B (grass)?
What happens to the water in box A (soil)?
Which jar contains the most water?

Can you find any places where this is occurring naturally?
What happens at these places during heavy rain?
What changes can you predict will occur at these places?

Moving in water

Look at your flood pictures (page 20).
What is being carried in the
flood water?

Half-fill a jar with water.
Mark the water level on the
side of the jar.

Put a piece of wood in the jar.
Does the wood float?
What happened to the water
level in the jar?

Push the wood under water.
What happens to the water level?
What happens when you release
the wood?
Try floating different things
in the jar.
Make a list of things that float.
Does a sponge float?

Place a marble in an empty tube.
Turn the tube upside down.
How fast does the marble move?
Fill the tube with water.
Cork it.
Turn the tube upside down.
How fast does the marble move?
What happens if you put an air
bubble in the tube?
Try different-shaped objects in the tube.
Try a coin, a screw and a piece of wood.

Wood block

Mark

Water

Water

Glass marble

Wave power

Look at the waves moving on a
large area of water.
How big are the waves?
Are they all the same size?
Which way do the waves break?
Which way is the wind blowing?
Do all the waves break at the
same place?

Look carefully at a wave. What happens to it?
What colour is the wave after it has broken?
Can you see air bubbles in the water?

Watch a small stone as several waves run over it.
What happens to the stone?
What happens to the sand or mud around the stone?

Stand in the water. Can you feel the force of the wave?
Have you ever tried body surfing on a breaking wave?
Have you ever watched surfers?
Where does the speed of their surf boards come from?

Have you ever seen sea defences?
Do you think a storm could break down these defences?

Moving water wears away land

Collect sand from a river or beach.
Rub your fingers through the sand.
Can you feel how rough the sand is?
Look through a lens at the sand grains.
What different-coloured grains can you see?
Can you see shell fragments?

Shake some sand in a jar of water.
Watch the sand settle.

Where are the pebbles in your river or beach?
What shape are the pebbles?
What made the pebbles smooth?
Can you find any pebbles the same colour as your
sand grains? Why is this?

Find a large rock in the river or beach.
How did the rock get there?
What is the water doing to the rock?

Can you see potholes in the rock?
What do you see inside the pothole?

Have you ever seen a waterfall?
The power of the falling water wears rock
away.

Pothole

Sand

Small
pebbles

Rock

Ice power

Fill an ice tray with water.
Is the water surface flat?
Put the tray in a freezer.
Which part of the water freezes first?
Is the ice surface flat?

Fill a small, screw-top glass bottle with water.
Screw the top on tightly.
Put the bottle inside a plastic bag. Seal the bag.
Put the bag in the freezer. What do you notice when
the water has turned to ice?
Does water take up more room when it freezes?
Water gets into cracks in rocks, then freezes and
splits the rock.

Put an ice cube in a jar of water. Does the ice float?
If ice is frozen water how can it float on water?
Where are icebergs found? How are they formed?

Glaciers are frozen rivers.
They have rocks frozen in them.
Rocks at the bottom of a glacier
scour out the glacier bed.

Water has dissolving power

Put ten spoonfuls of water in a jar.
Add a spoonful of rock salt or sea salt.
What happens to the salt?
Stir the water. What happens?
Taste the water. What does it taste like?
How many spoonfuls of salt can you
dissolve in the water?
Keep adding salt to the water. What happens?

Try dissolving all sorts of things in water.
Make a list of things that dissolve easily.

Leave a dish of salt water in a warm place.
What happens to the water? What is left behind?
Look at this with a lens. Taste it.

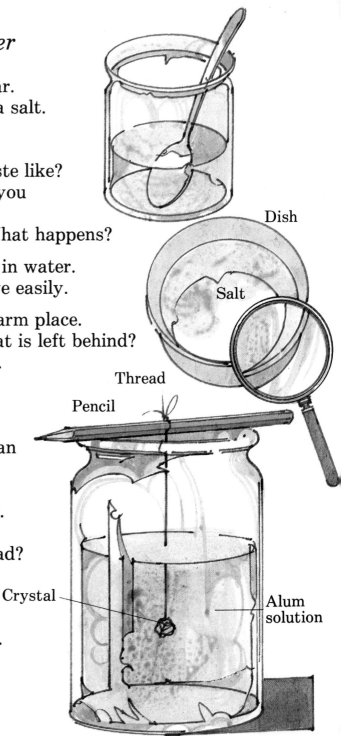

Dish

Salt

Thread

Pencil

Dissolve alum in water until no
more dissolves.
Pour the alum solution into a clean
jar.
Push a thread into the solution.
Tie the other end around a pencil.
After a day, lift out the thread.
Are crystals forming on the thread?
Remove all but one crystal.
Replace the thread.
Watch your crystal grow.
Always remove all other crystals.

Crystal

Alum
solution

You can also grow crystals from
rock salt and Epsom salt.

Caves and caverns

Water can make caves in many kinds of rock.
Sea water scours out caves in cliffs.
The largest caves are in soft rock such as chalk or limestone.

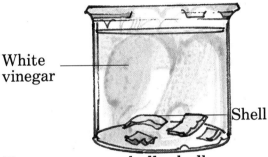

White vinegar

Shell

Put some sea shell, chalk or limestone in a jar. Cover it with white vinegar.
What happens? Shake the jar.
What happens to the shell, chalk or limestone?
River water dissolves carbon dioxide gas from the air. This makes the river acidic.
Decaying vegetation in the river also makes it acidic. This acid slowly dissolves away the chalk or limestone.
Stalactites and stalagmites are formed by drips of water evaporating slowly, rather like making a crystal.

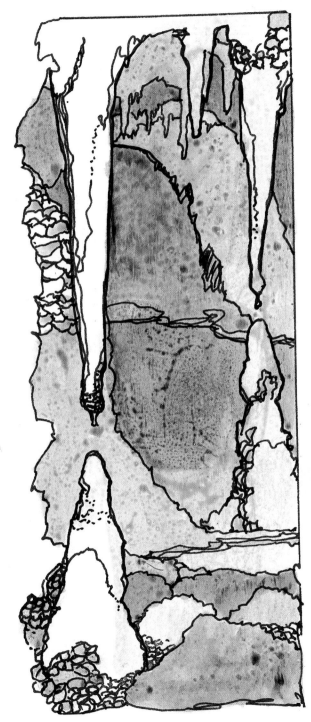

Chapter 5 Surface-tension power

Looking at water drops

Fill a clean tumbler with water until it is
nearly overflowing.
Look along the water surface.
Gently touch the water surface with a pencil.
What happens?
Touch the surface at the rim of the tumbler.
What happens?

Coin

Water to
top

Fill a tumbler with water until it is nearly
overflowing.
Slide a coin into the water.
What happens?
How many coins can you slide in before the
water overflows?

What shape are drops from a dripping tap?
What seems to hold them together?
What is the biggest drop you can make?

Put a drop of water on a table.
Look at it through a lens.
Put drops of water on all sorts of
things.
Try plastic, waxed card, paper and
newspaper.
What happens?
Put drops on different kinds of
cloth.
Try putting a drop onto a raincoat.
How does a raincoat keep out the
rain?

Surface-tension power

Make five small holes close together
in the base of a can.
Hold the can over a bowl and try to
fill the can with water.
Are the jets of water separate?
Twist the water together with your
fingers.
Do the jets stay twisted?

Put a clean 'camel-hair' paint brush
under water.
What do the bristles look like?
Slowly raise the brush out of the water.
What do the bristles look like now?

Pour water down a smooth, clean rod.
Does the water stay on the rod?

Use thin wood to make a boat.
Notch the stern.
Stick a piece of soap in the notch.
Put your boat in clean water.
What happens?

Put a small piece of camphor
instead of soap in the stern of your
boat.
Put your boat in clean water.
What happens?
Float a loop of cotton in clean water.
Add some detergent to the middle
of the loop.
What happens?

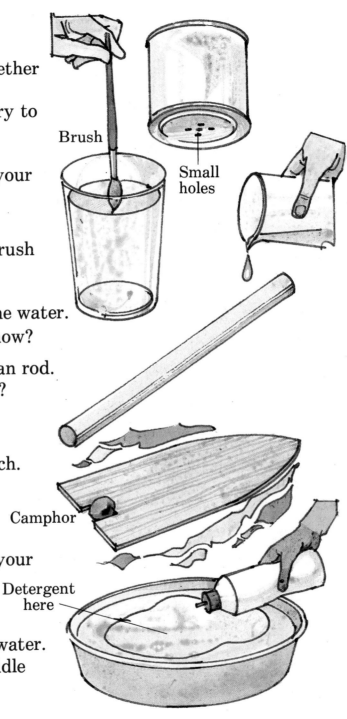

Brush

Small
holes

Camphor

Detergent
here

Water currents

Fill a glass jar with cold water.
Stand it in an empty bowl.
Fill another glass jar with warm water.
Put ink or food colouring in the warm water.
Notice how the colour mixes into the warm water.

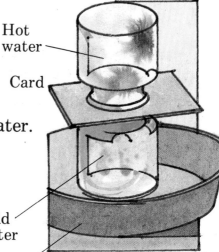

Hot water

Card

Cold water

Large bowl

Put a card over the warm water jar.
Hold the card in place and turn the warm jar
upside down over the cold jar.
Carefully, slip out the card.
What happens? Do the waters mix?

Do the experiment again, but this
time stand the warm water jar in
the bowl. Put the cold water jar on
the hot water jar. Slip out the card.
What happens?

Put some cold water in a clear, flame-proof dish.
Put some coloured bath crystals in the water.
Put the dish over a low heat.
Watch the water currents.

Crystals

In the summer, the water at the top of a lake is hotter
than at the bottom.
In the winter, the water at the top is colder. Ice forms
on the lake. This ice insulates the water from the
effects of cold winds.
There are plans to put water turbines in strong sea
currents to make electricity.

Water for life

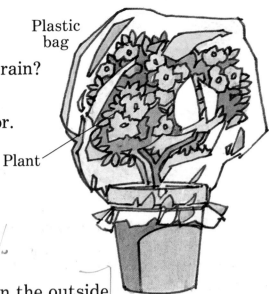

Plastic bag

Plant

What happens to water in puddles after rain?
Where does the water go?

Breathe out onto a cold window or mirror.
What can you see on the glass?

Put a plastic bag over a potted plant.
Leave it for a day.
What collects on the inside of the bag?
Where has it come from?

Put ice cubes in a can.
After a few minutes, what can you see on the outside
of the can?
Rub your finger on the outside of the can. What is <u>dew?</u>

Fill a clean bottle with hot water. Leave it for several
minutes.
Pour out nearly all the hot water.
Stand an ice cube on the top of the bottle.
What do you see forming in the air under the ice cube?
How do mist, fog and clouds form?

Clean water

Put clean blotting paper in the top of a jar.
Pour muddy water into the blotting paper.
What happens to the water?
What is left in the blotting paper?
What colour is the water in the jar?
This process is called filtering.

Our water is not pure. It has to be cleaned
before we can drink it.
Our waste water from home is purified
before it goes back into the river.
Clean water is essential for our lives.

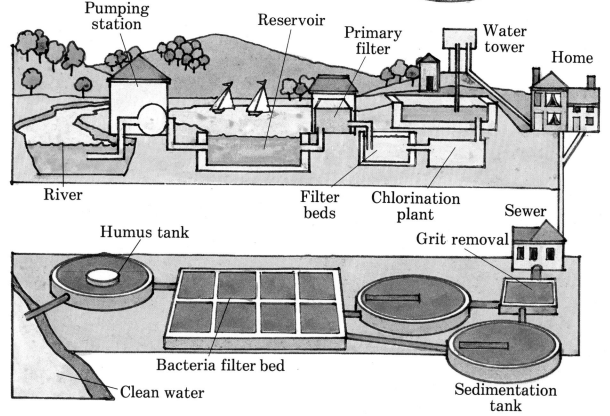